ENDANGERED
SAVANNAH ANIMALS

Dave Taylor

Toronto · Oxford · New York

Crabtree Publishing Company

ENDANGERED ANIMALS SERIES

Text and photographs by Dave Taylor

To Jim, who shared the adventure

Editor-in-chief
Bobbie Kalman

Editor
David Schimpky

Cover mechanicals
Rose Campbell

Design and computer layout
Antoinette "Cookie" DeBiasi

Separations and film
EC Graphics Ltd.

Printer
Worzalla Publishing

Published by
Crabtree Publishing Company

350 Fifth Avenue	360 York Road, RR4	73 Lime Walk
Suite 3308	Niagara-on-the-Lake	Headington
New York	Ontario, Canada	Oxford OX3 7AD
N.Y. 10118	L0S 1J0	United Kingdom

Cataloguing in Publication Data
Taylor, Dave, 1948-
  Endangered savannah animals

(The endangered animals series)
Includes index.
ISBN 0-86505-535-1 (library bound) ISBN 0-86505-545-9 (pbk.)
The special problems of the shrinking savannah and the animals that are sheltered in this small area are explored.

1. Grassland fauna - Africa - Juvenile literature. 2. Endangered species - Africa - Juvenile literature. 3. Wildlife conservation - Africa - Juvenile literature. I. Title. II. Series: Taylor, Dave, 1948- . The endangered animals series.

QL115.T39 1993   j591.96'0915'3   **LC93-6213**

Contents

The African savannah

The savannah, which covers a large area of the African continent, is one of the world's richest habitats for wild animals. Grassy areas surround clumps of trees, making the savannah look like a cross between a forest and a grassland. Some animals, such as the rhinoceros and the giraffe, prefer the more wooded parts of the savannah. Others, such as the lion and the zebra, like the more grassy parts. The elephant and the vulture live in both.

The existence of the savannah is in great danger. As a result, all the animals that make the savannah their home are in danger, too.

If savannah areas continue to disappear, unique animals, such as the Masai giraffes above, may be left without homes.

Hunting for sport and money

Savannah animals became endangered because they were overhunted in the past. When Europeans came to Africa, some hunted and killed these animals for sport. Others killed the wildlife for money. They sold elephant tusks and rhinoceros horns.

Ruthless poachers

The tusks were fashioned into jewelry, and the rhino horns were used to make dagger handles. When people realized that the number of animals was becoming dangerously low, laws were passed to protect them. Unfortunately, poachers still kill many savannah animals. Poachers are people who illegally hunt endangered animals for money.

Animals in the crossfire

When the Europeans settled in Africa, they claimed various territories for their countries. These territories were called **colonies**. About thirty years ago, most of the European countries that had African colonies gave the land back to the Africans. Unfortunately, the people of these ex-colonies did not always agree with their new leaders, and many wars broke out. In the course of this fighting, thousands of innocent people and animals were killed. The fighting continues in several countries today.

Habitat in danger

The most serious threat facing savannah animals is the loss of their habitat. Today much of the savannah has been changed into farmland. The animals are confined more and more to reserves and national parks, but even these parks may not be safe much longer. They are being threatened because the number of people in Africa increases each year. Experts expect the population to double in less than 20 years! In order to feed themselves, Africans may need to farm the land in the parks and reserves.

Animals in danger

In recent years people have forced many kinds of animals to struggle for survival. In the savannah, illegal hunting, farming, and the loss of wilderness areas have made life difficult and sometimes impossible for hundreds of animal species.

Worldwide conservation groups use various terms to describe animals in danger. Animals that are **extinct** have not been seen in the wild for over 50 years. Animals referred to as **endangered** are likely to die out if their situation is not improved. **Threatened** animals are endangered in some areas where they live. **Vulnerable** animals may become endangered if they continue to face certain problems. **Rare** animals are species with small populations that may be at risk.

A concern for all animals

There is reason to be concerned about all animals living in the wild. As the human population grows, less space and food are available for wild animals. There is hope, however. Thanks to conservation groups, many animals that once faced extinction are surviving in healthy numbers again.

Large herds of wildebeest once roamed the savannah. There are still some herds living in national parks. Outside these parks, however, wildebeest are becoming rare. The herds must migrate to find food and water, but the presence of farms and ranches on the savannah makes this difficult. As a result, during droughts, many wildebeest die of thirst because they cannot travel to faraway wells and springs.

The sable antelope

Female sables usually have only one young at a time, but sometimes twins are born to a mother. These sable twins enjoy grazing together.

Some types of antelopes live in forests; others live in grassland areas. The sable antelope enjoys the savannah, which is like both. It is usually found in grassland areas that are close to the woods. Sable antelopes are rare—even in the parks and sanctuaries of the savannah.

My territory!

Scientists have recently discovered that male sables are territorial. The same male may hold a territory for more than two years. Each male rounds up groups of 10 to 20 females and tries to keep them within his area for mating.

Sometimes males come together and clash over a territory. When they fight, both males go down on their knees and push against each other. They seldom get hurt. One bull soon gives up and leaves.

Aggressive fighters

Although antelopes live in herds of up to 100 animals, they find no safety in numbers. They are attacked by wild dogs, leopards, and lions. The sable antelope protects itself by being a very aggressive fighter. It uses its horns, which can be over five feet (1.5 meters) long. These impressive weapons have been known to keep lions away! Unfortunately, the antelope's horns have not kept away the hunters. In fact, hunters consider the horns prized trophies. The sable antelope is still hunted in some parts of Africa despite the fact that it is endangered.

An uncertain future

The giant sable antelope, which lives in Angola, is a subspecies of the sable antelope. It was the last of the large African animals to be discovered by scientists. This type of sable antelope has been legally protected since 1926, but there are fewer than 1000 left because of poaching. Government protection has not worked because very little money is being spent on conservation programs.

Height: 54 inches (137 centimeters)
Length: 6.5 feet (2 meters)
Weight: 450-580 pounds (204-263 kilograms)
Where it lives: From southern Kenya to parts of South Africa

The sable antelope's horns both help and hurt these animals. They provide the animal with excellent defense, but they also attract hunters who want the horns as trophies.

The gerenuk

The gerenuk is a strange-looking animal that has the body and coloring of an antelope but the long neck of a giraffe. In the Somali language, its name means "giraffe-necked," but this animal is actually a member of the gazelle family.

Future in jeopardy

Although gerenuks are not yet considered an endangered species, there is a growing concern for their welfare. Wars in Ethiopia and Somalia have claimed the lives of many of these unique animals. In Kenya, a growing need for farmland has taken away much of their grazing range. The time may soon come when the gerenuk is found only in national parks and reserves.

Picky eaters

The savannah is dry most of the year. In order to survive, gerenuks spend a lot of time looking for the tree leaves that make up their diet. These leaves provide them with both food and moisture.

Gerenuks feed on the leaves of over 80 kinds of trees. Their long necks help them reach the high branches, but that often isn't high enough. To reach even higher, the gerenuk stands up on its hind legs.

Breeding territories

The strongest male gerenuks claim territories and mark them with their scent glands. They chase out any male that challenges them, although they seldom fight. Within a territory a male gerenuk mates with all the females that are ready to breed.

Time to give birth

When it is time to give birth, the mother gerenuk selects a secluded spot to have her baby. If the baby is a female, it will stay in the same area as its mother until it matures. On the other hand, young males leave their mother and wander alone until they feel strong enough to challenge a territorial male.

Height: 43-58 inches (109-147 centimeters)
Length: 55-65 inches (140-165 centimeters)
Weight: 63-114 pounds (28-52 kilograms)
Where it lives: Kenya, Ethiopia, and Somalia

Since they seldom drink water, juicy leaves are the major source of moisture for the gerenuk.

Giraffes

Ever since the giraffe was first seen outside Africa, it has held a special place in the hearts of people. The Chinese first saw a giraffe in 1414, when one was brought to the emperor's court. They thought it was a god! Giraffes were not brought to Europe until 1827. When one arrived at a zoo in Paris, France, people traveled from all over to marvel at it.

Two kinds of giraffes

There are nine species of giraffes living on the savannah. Two of them are endangered: the reticulated giraffe and the Rothchild's giraffe. The reticulated giraffe has spots on its legs, whereas the legs of the Rothchild's giraffe are creamy white. Another difference is that the reticulated giraffe has up to five horns; the Rothchild's giraffe has no more than four.

Busy eaters

Giraffes like to **browse**, which means they feed on leaves. They spend up to 20 hours each day eating! In a week, giraffes consume hundreds of pounds of leaves from their favorite tree, the acacia. They use their 18-inch (46-centimeter) tongue to pull the branches toward them so they can reach the leaves.

Powerful necks

Giraffes use their head and horns for fighting. The giraffe's head and neck are very heavy. Together they weigh about 550 pounds (250 kilograms). When fighting, giraffes stand side by side and swing their long necks at each other.

Each one uses its head to thump into the opponent's neck. Scientists call this behavior "necking." Young giraffes often engage in playful necking, but a heavy blow from an adult can cause a lot of damage to an enemy!

Dangerous times

When a baby giraffe is born, its mother is standing up. The calf starts out life with a five-foot (1.5-meter) drop to the ground. For the first month or so, the young giraffe's mother nurses it and keeps a close eye on it. After that, the calf is left to fend for itself in a nursery herd from dawn to dusk while its mother wanders off in search of food. During this time, seven out of ten calves are killed by predators. Each night the mother returns and stays close to her calf. Mother giraffes nurse their young for almost a year.

Limited to parks

At present about 400 reticulated giraffes live in the Samburu Game Reserve in Kenya and a few thousand live outside this park, mostly in other reserves. There are fewer than 200 Rothchild's giraffes in Kenya and less than 900 in Uganda. The survival of all giraffes that live outside protected parks is uncertain due to overhunting and habitat loss.

Height: 11-17 feet (3.5-5.2 meters)
Weight: 1200-4250 pounds (544-1928 kilograms)
Where they live: Uganda and Kenya

The giraffe above is a Rothchild's giraffe. Its legs are a creamy white color. Giraffes do not live in stable herds. Females and males move from one group to another, seldom staying in the same group for more than a day or two.

The giraffe on the right is a reticulated giraffe. You can tell because its legs are spotted. All giraffes are equipped with horns. These horns are different from the horns of other animals because they are part of the bone of the skull. The horns are covered with thick hide and hair.

The Cape buffalo

The Cape buffalo, which is also called the African buffalo, prefers the wooded parts of the savannah. It doesn't browse on trees as giraffes do. It is strictly a grass eater, or **grazer**.

Herd life

Cape buffalo live in herds of up to several thousand animals. Herds provide young buffalo with protection and knowledge about such things as migration routes and feeding spots. The basic unit in a herd is a female and her calf. Female buffalo usually stay in the herd into which they were born, but males often leave and join another herd. There are usually several adult bulls in a herd.

Dangerous horns

Cape buffalo have an effective defense against predators—their horns. Both sexes of buffalo have horns, but the male's are bigger. Thanks to these weapons, a herd of buffalo is reasonably safe from a predator's attack. When danger is detected, the bulls quickly move forward to confront the enemy. Even lions stay away from these buffalo. As a result, buffalo can live up to 18 years if they avoid predators and accidents.

Watch out!

Sometimes older male buffalo leave the herd and wander the savannah alone. A lone bull buffalo is an animal that should be treated with caution. Lone males have been known to challenge animals much larger than themselves, such as elephants and rhinos. They have even charged tourist vehicles!

A deadly disease

The Cape buffalo almost disappeared in the late nineteenth century, when a disease called **rinderpest** arrived in Africa. Rinderpest is a virus carried by domestic cattle. It was a common disease in Asia and Europe but was unknown in Africa until 1890, when European cattle were first brought to Ethiopia. By 1896 the disease had spread as far south as South Africa. Rinderpest affected many of the wild herds of the savannah, which had no resistance to the disease. The effect on the Cape buffalo was especially deadly because they are closely related to domestic cattle.

An uncertain future

Scientists finally found a way of controlling the deadly disease in the 1960s. Unfortunately, by then the great herds of Cape buffalo were gone. There were none left in South Africa except for a few herds in parks and reserves. In other areas, the buffalo survived in isolated pockets. Today their numbers are recovering, and there are even some herds containing thousands of animals roaming the savannah.

Height: 6 feet (1.8 meters)
Length: 6.9-9.8 feet (2.1-3 meters)
Weight: 1102-2000 pounds (500-907 kilograms)
Where it lives: Throughout southern Africa

Much of the former range of the Cape buffalo has been turned into farmland. If its habitat continues to disappear, this animal's survival will be in serious jeopardy.

(above) Rhinoceros horns are made of a tissue similar to the tissue found in horse hoofs and human fingernails. Poachers cut off the horns and sell them to people in the Middle East and Asia.
(below) Black rhinos are usually accompanied by small birds that help them stay clean. These birds eat the insects and parasites that make their home on the rhino's thick skin.

The black rhinoceros

Of all the animals in this book, the black rhinoceros is the first one likely to become extinct in the wild, despite tremendous efforts to preserve this animal.

Lone animals

Black rhinos are not territorial, but they do have a well-defined home range. They seem to have a regular routine, often following the same paths from one place to another. Rhinos usually prefer to be alone, although occasionally they come together for a short time in pairs or small groups of four or five animals. The exception is a female and her calf, who stay together for up to four years.

Food, water, and mud

Rhinos are browsers, seeking their food from the savannah's trees and shrubs. In the forest they find food easily but, in open areas, the rhino has to travel far to find enough to eat. Rhinos usually go to a river or watering hole each day. During droughts, however, they can survive on the moisture they get from the shrubs they eat. Black rhinos love a good mud bath and spend hours wallowing. The mud covering protects their skin from the hot sun and bothersome insects.

Dangerous neighbors

In the early 1900s large parts of Africa were being settled. People did not want rhinos to wander onto their properties because they believed these animals to be extremely dangerous. By the mid-1960s rhinos were killed off over much of their range, and by 1984 the rhino population in Africa was down to 9000. Today there are fewer than 3000 black rhinoceros left.

Hunted for horns

Although it is now known that rhinos pose little threat to people, these animals are still in danger because people are willing to pay high prices for their horns. Poachers hunt rhinos illegally, cut off their horns, and sell them in the Middle East. There, the horns are made into prized dagger handles for the wealthy.

No horn is better than one!

In Zimbabwe, wildlife managers are cutting off the horns of rhinos so that poachers will not kill these animals. In many countries, armed patrols are ordered to "shoot to kill" illegal hunters. Poachers, however, will even risk death for the large amount of money they can earn by selling a rhino horn.

In North America and Europe, conservation groups have raised public awareness and money to help save the black rhinoceros. Unfortunately, there are too few rhinos left in too large an area to properly protect these animals from poachers. Unless a better way is found to guard the rhinoceros, its future will continue to be in jeopardy.

Height: 63 inches (160 centimeters)
Length: 10-12 feet (3-3.65 meters)
Weight: 2200-4000 pounds (1000-1814 kilograms)
Where it lives: From Somalia to South Africa

Zebras

Zebras are closely related to horses. If you look, you can see the family resemblance. Male zebras are called **stallions**, the females are called **mares**, and the young are known as **foals**.

The most obvious difference between horses and zebras is the stripes of zebras. Scientists aren't sure why zebras have stripes. Most believe that it helps zebras identify one another.

Different species

Two kinds of zebras living on the savannah are the plains zebra and the Grevy's zebra. The biggest difference between these two is how they interact with other members of their own species.

The plains zebra

Plains zebras live in herds consisting of a stallion, seven or eight mares, and their foals. Scientists have learned some surprising facts about the social structure of these herds. The stallion is a very devoted mate and father. When a predator chases a stallion's small herd, the male stays at the back to protect his females and young. It is not unusual for a stallion to lose his life while he is protecting his family!

A female plains zebra usually has a foal every year of her life. The herd stallion stands guard during the birth to protect the mare from predators.

The Grevy's zebra

The Grevy's zebra has a different lifestyle. It does not live in herds. Instead, the strongest stallions have large territories. Other males within these territories must obey the leader or be chased away. The territorial stallion is the only one allowed to mate with the females in the territory.

Although groups of Grevy's zebras occasionally graze together, the group is not an organized herd. The only strong relationship among Grevy's zebras is between a mare and her foal. Together, they move throughout different territories.

Migration made difficult

Much of the zebra's range has been taken over by agriculture. Herds of cattle over-graze areas where zebras look for food, and fenced-in ranches and farms prevent zebras from migrating. These factors have caused zebra populations to drop. As a result, fewer than 7000 Grevy's zebras exist in the wild.

Grevy's zebra
Length: 8-8.5 feet (2.5-2.6 meters)
Weight: 771-950 pounds (350-430 kilograms)
Where it lives: Somalia, Ethiopia, and Kenya

Plains zebra
Length: 6-8 feet (1.9-2.45 meters)
Weight: 385-780 pounds (175-355 kilograms)
Where it lives: From Somalia to South Africa

(opposite top) When farms are fenced in on the open savannah, zebras find it difficult to reach watering holes such as this one. (opposite bottom) The Grevy's zebra is bigger than the plains zebra, has a more horselike face, and larger ears. Its stripes are narrow and do not cover its belly. Grevy's zebras live in the desert-like areas of the savannah.

The African elephant

The plight of the African elephant has become well known in recent years. It is sad that this magnificent species should come so close to extinction. There is good news, however. It now appears that the African elephant may survive into the next century.

Beautiful tusks

Tusks are the elephant's long teeth, which are made of a material called **ivory**. They are valued as material for carving and for making jewelry. People have been hunting the elephant for its tusks for thousands of years. The real slaughter, however, did not start until the beginning of the twentieth century. Hunters realized that a lot of money could be earned in the ivory trade. Their modern weapons made the killing of elephants safe and easy.

Doomed to extinction?

In 1930 it was estimated that Africa was home to as many as ten million elephants. By 1976 that number had dropped to a little over one million. Ten years later, only half that number were left. Many people feared that these majestic animals were doomed to extinction.

Slaughtered by poachers

In 1989 the African elephant was declared endangered. In 1990 most of the countries around the world banned the trade of ivory in order to save the elephant. Despite the ban, poachers have continued to kill elephants illegally for their ivory.

Stopping the killing

Some African countries have tried extra measures to save elephants. Botswana and Zimbabwe, two countries with large elephant populations, are now giving some of the tourist money from park visits to help the local people. Most of that money, as well as the meat and hide of legally hunted elephants, goes to the surrounding communities. People who depended on poaching for a living now find that living elephants are more valuable than dead ones!

Kenya helps elephants

The East African country of Kenya was one of the main supporters of a complete ban on the ivory trade, but poaching continued there, too. In 1989 the president appointed Dr. Richard Leakey, a world-famous anthropologist, to attack the problem. Leakey began by raising funds to help arm park rangers against poaching gangs. He raised the rangers' pay and fired corrupt officials, replacing them with trusted ones. By 1991 fewer than fifteen elephants were killed in six months!

Height: 10.5 feet (3.2 meters)
Length: 10-13 feet (3-4 meters)
Weight: 2000-13,000 pounds (907-6000 kilograms)
Where it lives: Kenya and southern Africa

Consumers in North America and Europe helped save the elephant by refusing to buy ivory goods and by campaigning for the ivory trade ban. As a result of these worldwide efforts, elephant herds are well on their way to recovery, and the danger of extinction is no longer in the near future.

The leopard

Not long ago leopards could be found all over Africa. Today the species is almost extinct in North Africa. Although leopards are still fairly common on the savannah, their population has dropped as their habitat has been destroyed by loggers and farmers.

Besides the savannah, leopards live in habitats such as tropical forests, dense jungles, scrub deserts, and mountainous areas. They are the most widespread of all the big cats. In most of these areas, they have few natural enemies other than human beings.

Secretive cats

No one knows for certain how many leopards there are because these cats are active at night and stay out of view. On the savannah, leopards make use of the trees for hiding. Their spotted coats offer perfect camouflage, especially when they are hunting in the shadowy cover of the forest.

Solitary hunters

Leopards are solitary hunters; they never assist one another in hunting the way lions do. These cats usually hide until a victim walks by and then pounce on it. Leopards may share overlapping home ranges, but they avoid other leopards. They need a large range in order to hunt enough food, but they stay away from the open grasslands of the savannah. Lions hunt there and have been known to kill and eat leopards.

Food in storage

Leopards are **carnivores**; they only eat meat. They dine on small mammals, birds, and larger animals such as impala and young wildebeest. If a leopard kills something that it cannot eat all at once, it carries the leftovers into a tree for storage. Hiding the food keeps it safe from other predators such as lions and hyenas, which cannot climb trees.

A leopard and its spots

There are several kinds of leopards that live on the savannah. They are all spotted, even the black leopards. Black leopards, which are also called black panthers, are quite common in more forested areas. If you look carefully at a black panther, you can see that it, too, has spots.

Made into coats

For years, leopards were hunted for their fur, which was made into coats for wealthy women. Today the demand for leopard fur has dropped because fur coats are no longer as fashionable. Some poaching still takes place, however.

Height: 18-32 inches (45-81 centimeters)
Length: 5-10 feet (1.5-3 meters)
Weight: 62-200 pounds (28-90 kilograms)
Where it lives: Throughout Africa

(left) Recent studies have found that leopards can live around African towns and villages without being detected. They survive in patches of forest by feeding on small animals. Occasionally, they even eat dogs and cats!

The lion

There is not much danger that lions will become extinct in the near future because many of these cats are living and breeding in zoos. In the wild, however, there are few places outside parks where lions are are able to exist in truly natural environments. At one time, lions were among the most widespread of all carnivores, but now they are found in healthy numbers only in African parks.

Life in the pride

Lions are the world's only social cat. Unlike leopards and tigers, who like to be alone, lions usually live in groups called **prides**. Each pride is led by a male lion but, after two or three years, his leadership can be challenged by a younger lion. If the challenge is successful, the older lion must leave.

Lionesses are the heart of the pride and stay with the group throughout their lives. They are usually related to one another as sisters, daughters, and nieces.

Food for the pride

Although they may hunt together to bring down a zebra, wildebeest, or buffalo, lions do not share their food. Male lions chase female lions away from a kill, and females chase away cubs. There has to be a lot of meat to feed the entire pride!

Tough life for cubs

Female lions have an average of three cubs in a litter. When the cubs are young, they are in danger of being killed by hyenas, leopards, and other male lions that may take over a pride. When they are older, however, they have no natural enemies other than people. The cubs are introduced to the pride when they are six weeks old. They are nursed until they are a year old. After that, the cubs must fight for their food with the rest of the pride.

Out on their own

Male lions leave the pride when they are three or four years old. They wander the savannah on their own, and many never join another pride. The strongest males will eventually challenge males that rule a pride for the right to take it over.

Survival tied to others

When the big herds of zebra and wildebeest migrate to seek water, life is often hard for lions. These cats are territorial and cannot follow the herds, so they are forced to eat smaller animals that do not migrate. Sometimes half the cubs starve to death during these times.

The future of Africa's lions is tied to the future of the savannah's great herds. If African nations do not set aside large reserves where wildebeest and zebras are free to roam, the lions will soon disappear.

Height: 3.3-4 feet (1-1.2 meters)
Length: (with tail) Up to 11 feet (3.5 meters)
Weight: Up to 550 pounds (250 kilograms)
Where it lives: Throughout the savannah

Sometimes lions are poached for their teeth, claws, and hides, which are sold to tourists as souvenirs of their trip to Africa.

(above) Even though female lions do most of the hunting, males are good hunters, too. Male lions protect the pride's territory and keep out unwanted males. (below) Fighting is common among lions. The only way a lion can get enough food is by being tough and bullying its way in to feed.

Vultures

The vulture is a common sight on the savannah. It sits along riverbanks, roosts in trees, and soars in the sky, waiting for a meal. This bird has a hooked beak and clawed feet, features that are left over from a time when its ancestors hunted for food. Most of Africa's vultures, however, never hunt. Their survival depends on finding dead animals to eat. Vultures find food near areas such as national parks, where there are large herds of animals. These birds are important to the ecosystem because they help clean up the savannah.

Eating in order

There are six different species of vultures on the African savannah. Each has its own special place in the feeding order. The first vultures that arrive at a carcass are the lappet-faced and the white-headed vultures. They have strong beaks and are the only vultures that can open up a carcass. The white-backed and griffon vultures are the next to feed. They can poke their heads right into the dead animal's body cavity. Their necks are bare so that the blood can be easily cleaned off. If the blood were to stay on their necks, it might cause diseases. The last birds to feed are the hooded and Egyptian vultures. They eat the scraps.

Effective flyers

Vultures soar over the savannah, searching for dead animals. In a day, they may cover hundreds of miles before they find food. They have developed a unique way of flying that uses little energy.

Each morning, these birds wait for the sun to heat the land. Vultures use the hot air that rises from the earth to carry them high up into the sky. These warm winds are called **thermals**.

Keen eyesight

Vultures have excellent eyesight, and their bird's-eye view often enables them to be the first scavengers to arrive at a dead animal. A vulture can also spot other vultures at a carcass miles away and join in the feast. When vultures cannot find food, they live off stored fat in their bodies.

Fewer vultures around

Vultures were once found in large numbers in southern Europe and the Middle East. Today, they have all but vanished from these areas. In Africa, vultures are still quite common, but their future is in danger. Vultures depend on the great herds of the savannah for food. As the herds disappear from the land, the prime source of the vulture's food also vanishes. The vulture's survival is tied to the survival of other savannah animals.

Length: 26-40 inches (66-101 centimeters)
Weight: 4-8 pounds (1.8-3.6 kilograms)
Where they live: Africa and parts of Europe

(opposite top) When vultures find a carcass, they wait for a while until the carcass has rotted in the sun before they eat it. (opposite left) Egyptian vultures are the last to feed and pick up the scraps. There are rarely more than two of these birds at a kill. (opposite right) The vulture perched in the bush is a white-backed vulture.

Preserving the savannah

There was a time when people thought the savannah and its wildlife would survive forever. Today we know how fragile this ecosystem really is. Much of the savannah is being farmed and, as Africa's population grows, even more farmland will be needed. The entire savannah may eventually disappear.

Organizations that help

If this rich ecosystem is to be preserved, everyone must help. There are some organizations that help fund national parks and anti-poaching patrols. These groups help stop the senseless slaughter of protected species. Other organizations educate and train people in the latest farming techniques. Teaching Africans better farming methods helps them produce more food on less land. You and your parents may wish to research these organizations and make a donation.

Support wild Africa!

African nations are very poor and cannot afford to make conservation programs a top priority. In order to help Africans protect their wildlife, richer nations are helping out by providing African conservation groups with money, teachers, and volunteers. If you think this is a good idea, write to a politician and let him or her know that you support this cause.

Savannah animals, such as the wildebeest on the opposite page and the zebras above, are losing their habitat to humans. You can see how the city in the background may soon spread to the area on which the zebras are now grazing.

Go to the zoo

Most modern zoos try to recreate the natural homes of savannah animals. Lions, zebras, and giraffes can roam savannah-like areas. These zoos help rescue endangered species by allowing them to live and breed in safety. When you visit such a zoo, you are showing interest and support for all animals.

Take a trip

Encourage your family, friends, and neighbors to visit the savannah. Their tourist dollars will help pay the costs of saving wild animals, and their visit will show the local people how important their conservation work is. When you are older, you may even wish to go to Africa and work for a conservation group!

Glossary

anthropologist A scientist who studies the development of the human race

ban The official forbidding of something

browse To eat leaves and twigs

camouflage An animal's behavior or appearance that helps it hide by blending into its surroundings

carcass The dead body of an animal

carnivore Any animal with sharp teeth and claws that feeds on other animals

colony A territory that is controlled by a distant country

conservation Protection from loss, harm, or waste, especially of natural resources, such as wildlife

ecosystem A community of living things that are connected to one another and to the surroundings in which they live

endangered To be threatened with extinction

environment The setting and conditions in which a living being exists

extinct Not in existence; not seen in the wild for over 50 years

habitat The natural environment of a plant or animal

herd A group of animals that lives together

ivory The material that makes up elephant, walrus, and narwhal tusks

jeopardy Danger of loss, injury, or death

Middle East An area that includes parts of southwestern Asia, Turkey, Arabia, and northeastern Africa

migration The act of moving from one area to another

national park An area of land maintained for public use by the government

nurse To feed a baby with mother's milk

poacher A person who hunts animals illegally

population The people or animals of an area; the total number of individuals living in a particular area

predator An animal that kills and eats other animals

prey An animal that is hunted for food by another animal

pride A group of lions

reserve An area set aside for the protection of wildlife

rinderpest A cattle disease that originated in Europe and Asia

savannah A grassland characterized by scattered trees and shrubs

scavenger A creature that eats dead animals

scrub Low trees or bushes

species A group of related plants or animals that can produce young together

subspecies A group of animals within a species

territorial Relating to a territory

threatened Describing an animal that is endangered in some parts of its habitat

tropical Hot and humid; describing an area close to the equator

tusk A long, projecting, pointed tooth

vulnerable Capable of becoming endangered

wallow To roll about in mud or water

Index

5 6 7 8 9 0 Printed in USA 2 1 0 9 8 7